HELP, HOPE AND HAPPINESS

Libby Rees

AULTBEA
PUBLISHING LTD

Published by Aultbea Publishing, Inverness

Help, Hope and Happiness

First published in Great Britain by
Aultbea Publishing Company in 2005,
28 Church Street, Inverness IV1 1HB

Third Edition

ISBN 1905517025

Printed by Highland Printers Limited
Henderson Road, Inverness IV1 1SP

To Mum, who has always encouraged me
to follow my dreams.

Foreword

I wrote this book because I know from experience that it helps to realise you are not alone in having to deal with problems. I wanted to share with other children my ways of dealing with life.

Synopsis

This book is packed with original ideas on how to lead a more positive and successful life. So take a look inside and be inspired ......

I have had some pretty big issues to deal with, even though I am only 9 years old. I hope that you find this book useful and encouraging. I would also like to help lots of children believe in themselves.

For every copy of 'Help, Hope and Happiness' sold, we have chosen to make a donation to Save the Children to help their fight for children in the UK and around the world who suffer from poverty, disease, injustice and violence.

Nominated Charity:

 **Save the Children**

Biography

Libby Rees submitted her first manuscript aged only nine! The incredibly mature insight this author displays into the problems faced by the average child of today is quite simply astounding.

Libby is currently a student at a small New Forest primary school. When Libby is not occupied with her studies or her writing she likes to play her guitar. Libby loves all animals and always takes good care of her pet rabbit and goldfish. Otherwise, not surprisingly, she can be found engrossed in a riveting book.

Take a Break

Try to find some time to be alone. Enjoy a favourite film or book. This will give you some valuable time off from worrying, also it will help you relax. When you have had a decent break you will feel happier, more refreshed and able to cope with any problems you may have.

Special Phrase

Think of a funny phrase which always makes you laugh! Say it to yourself when you are feeling sad and it will cheer you up. My Mum and I listened to the taped story "Cliffhanger" by Jacqueline Wilson. In it one of the characters had a knitted toy and some bullies teased him by saying it was a "pink willie." Although we did not like the bullies, the thought of a knitted toy that looks like a pink willie never fails to make us laugh. So "pink willie" has become our special phrase.

Positive Thinking

Whenever anything happens try to look for the positive aspects. You have probably heard the saying "Every cloud has a silver lining". Well, if you look hard enough you can find something good in even the worst of situations. Try looking in the mirror first thing in the morning and say out loud to yourself "I am better and better every day!" five times. Trust me, I've done it and you really will start to feel more positive about your life.

An Achievement

Find something that you fear and try to overcome it, say for instance handling a spider (start with a really small one; not a Tarantula). This sense of achievement will encourage you to take on other challenges in your life and to realise you have an inner strength. You can also achieve something academically. By focussing on what you want to accomplish, you will have a much better chance of succeeding.

TGI Night

TGI stands for Thank God It's ----------- then you fill in the day of the week which is good for you to have as a special night. It could be Friday because it is the end of the school week or maybe Tuesday because your favourite TV programme is on. It's up to you but by having a special night to look forward to it will help you get through from week to week.

Review Your Week

Take some time out to review the week just gone and decide what worked well as well as what was a problem for you. Then think about how you could change the outcome to suit you best and plan the following week ahead using your new strategies. Think hard about what you want to achieve and you're half way there.

Let it All Out

Find a place where you can be all alone and let it all out – scream, shout, stamp your feet, whatever you feel like doing but this physical activity will help you release all the anger inside. Throwing is really good for this. Find a heap of sticks or stones and plenty of space. Next, for every stone or stick that you throw, shout out something that is bugging you as you launch them into the air. Afterwards you will feel much calmer.

Join a Club

Sometimes you could really use something to divert your brain, so joining a club will help you to forget your problems and find something new you can enjoy doing. A language club is a good idea or a sports club which will make you healthier as well. It is also a way of proving to yourself that you have the power and motivation to bring about changes in your life.

Pick a Project

Engross yourself in a project of your choice. It might be something you studied at school that you want to find out more about or just a topic that takes your fancy. You might consider making something as your project rather than a written task or try to gain a practical skill like cooking that you could use in the future.

Healthy Body, Healthy Mind

If you exercise, your body releases something called endorphins into your system. They rush around screaming out "Hey, we are feeling just great!" and they convince all the other parts of your body, including your brain, that you are fit to cope with anything the world throws at you. So get out there and get fit.

Two Words — "RETAIL THERAPY!"

Save up some money – it doesn't have to be much. Set yourself a shopping challenge by looking for something really special and good value for money. Don't spend all your money at once in the first shop you go to! This exercise will help you to focus on something different, give you plenty of exercise as you walk around the shops (take the phrase – shop 'til you drop – literally). This is also a great way to stimulate the creative part of your brain by taking in all the colours and designs.

Spic and Span

You may think to tidy your room is a chore! But, if you have a good clear out it can really put you back on track. It will be much easier to find things and will get rid of the clutter, so will avoid those frustrating hunts for your favourite T-shirt. Apply the same logic to your school bag and pencil case, then you will be ready for a fresh new start.

Get Out and About

Stuck at home you will feel more tired, frustrated and lazy than ever before. Try to get outdoors even if it is just in your garden. The fresh air will revive you and you will start to feel healthier. Work out a short route that you can walk in say 15 to 20 minutes. This will give you some time without distractions to think about how to resolve your problems, so try and fit this in 2 or 3 times a week.

Extra Effort

Try to make that extra effort to be kind to the people around you and you will find that you will strengthen your friendships and relationships. If you do this you will notice that more people like you and you will be able to like yourself even more.

Adopt a Pet

If possible find a pet for your own home that will be your sole responsibility. It can be anything, from an ant to an elephant, just as long as you will be taking care of it. If you can't have a pet in your home, then try asking a neighbour or relative if you can share the task of looking after their pet with them. By doing this you will be rewarded with an unselfish pleasure in caring for the needs of your chosen animal.

Write a Book

Find a small journal or notebook to record all of your worries and negative thoughts. By writing them down on paper you are transferring them from your mind. When the book is full, don't refer back to it but wait until it is Guy Fawkes' night and throw it onto the bonfire. This will prove to yourself, when the book is in flames, that the problems are also consumed by the fire.

(Do be careful around the fire!)

Work Your Socks Off!

The more effort you put into a project you will find the better the result turns out to be. You will get more satisfaction and take more pride from doing something really well, to the best of your ability, than if you do something badly and achieve a poor result. It is far nicer to be praised than to be told you are not working at the level you could be.

Daily Deed

Look out for opportunities to do something for somebody else in your life. Perhaps there is a person that does a lot for you and you can repay them in some way by doing a small task or helping them, for instance laying the table, clearing the dishes or trying to get on with your brothers or sisters.

Worry Wart

Stop getting worked up about what other people think. They probably will like you a lot more if you just relax and be yourself. If they are true friends they will like you for the way you are and if they don't then they are not the kind of companions you need.

Rock 'n' Roll Rota

Make a weekly rota and make sure you squeeze in time for yourself. By planning things out in advance you can make the most of your free time. Perhaps you have a diary or a planner to jot down your rota or if you are a whiz at IT you might do this on the computer.

Cookies or Cakes

Get creative in the kitchen. Some day you will have to cook for yourself, so why not start now and learn some of the basic skills you might need. It is very satisfying when you produce a tasty dish on your own that you can then share with others. There is a part of all of us that needs to satisfy our creative needs and this is a fun way of doing so. (Remember to check with an adult before you begin.)

Happy Tracks

Look through your music collection and find some tracks that you associate with happy memories or tunes that always make you want to get down and boogie! You will be surprised at how quickly your mood can be lifted and how suddenly you become energised.

Snap Shots

Look through your photo albums and linger over the snaps that show a good day out or event. Close your eyes for a few seconds and recall all the positive and blissful moments you have previously experienced.

A Problem Shared is a Problem Halved

Confide in your dearest friend. By putting your thoughts into words, saying them out loud to a friend and discussing your options, instantly things will seem easier. You may even find that your friend has had similar anxieties and will be able to support you.

Sweet Dreams

If you have had a good night's rest then you will be better able to face the world. Avoid eating late at night, especially cheese and baked beans (enough said!) as this will cause digestion activity to keep you tossing and turning in bed. Before you go to sleep try and focus on something relaxing. You may also find reading helpful.

Watch a Really Sad Movie

If you sit down to watch a movie which is really emotional and moving it is like turning a key in a lock – all your bottled up feelings will be released and you will feel so much better. Our bodies are designed to show emotion and by the physical act of crying you will find relief. (Have the tissues handy!)

Look and Feel Your Best

Whether it is getting ready to go to school each day or something fun like meeting your friends at the weekend, make sure you prepare well. It is nice to get dressed up in your finest things because it makes you feel good. Even if you have to wear a school uniform, you can make sure your hair is in a sassy style or that you have accessorised your bag, pencil case etc… to the max!

Beat the Badness

There is always somebody worse off than you are! Honest, believe me, just watch the news and you will find lots of things that are happening all over the world which are disastrous for hundreds of people. Be thankful that you are not caught up in something as terrible as a war or a famine or a tsunami.

Make a Difference

Fight World Poverty! Or take up some other challenge to help a charitable cause. This will give you a real buzz and even if there are things you are not able to change instantly about your own life, you will be able to make a difference elsewhere.

Carpe Diem – Seize the Day

Bit of Latin for you, if you have not seen the film "Dead Poets' Society" then watch it. The message in the film is to make the most of every day and every chance that comes your way. You don't want to look back at your life as a series of missed opportunities.